GOD IS...

Also available from Marshall Pickering *by Roy Mitchell:*

Gaberdine Swine
God Is . . . Theology for cats and other creatures

GOD IS...

Advanced Theology
for cats
and other creatures

Cartoons by
Roy Mitchell

Volume Two

MarshallPickering
An Imprint of HarperCollins*Publishers*

Marshall Pickering
An imprint of HarperCollins*Religious*
Part of HarperCollins*Publishers*
77-85 Fulham Palace Road, London W6 8JB

First published in Great Britain
by Marshall Pickering 1991

Printed and bound in Great Britain by
HarperCollins Manufacturing, Glasgow

A catalogue record for this book
is available from the British Library

GOD IS....

...CAPTAIN **AND** NAVIGATOR

GOD IS...

... ABLE TO GIVE YOU A
FRESH START

GOD IS...

...MY POWER SUPPLY

GOD IS......

Are you **sure** you don't mind me telling you all my problems?

... A **GOOD** LISTENER

GOD IS...

... RELIABLE

GOD IS....

... ABLE TO DEAL
WITH YOUR FEARS

GOD IS........

that was close!

... ALWAYS ON TARGET

GOD IS....

...IMAGINATIVE

GOD IS....

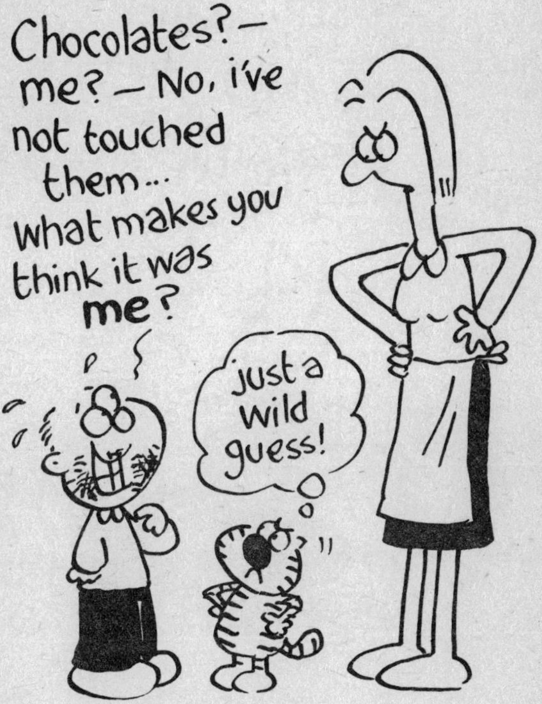

...**ALWAYS** TRUTHFUL

GOD IS...

...SOMETIMES WANTING US TO **MOVE**

GOD IS...

Can't stop— must dash—
I've got a church meeting
at 7.15 .... choir practise
at 8.30 ... Bible study group
                    at 9.15...

what's
the rush?
slow down!

...SOMETIMES WANTING
US TO BE **STILL**

GOD IS......

I got it **right** that time! — Thanks, Lord!

... PLEASED WHEN WE SUCCEED

GOD IS......

...ALWAYS READY TO SPEND TIME WITH US

GOD IS....

... HERE TODAY **AND** HERE TOMORROW

GOD IS...

...NOT A DICTATOR

GOD IS...

...PROLIFIC

GOD IS....

...THE SILVER LINING IN THE CLOUD

GOD IS....

...THE OIL IN MY LAMP

GOD IS...

Who, **me**? - you're joking! - I **can't**!

I'm too **busy**! - Have you any idea how **full** my schedule is?

I've got a lot on, too!

... NOT INTERESTED IN EXCUSES

GOD IS...

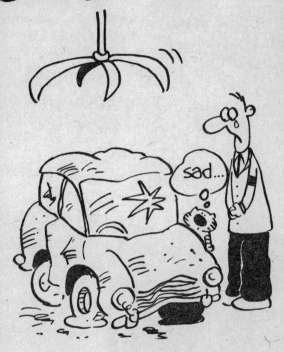

...EVERLASTING

GOD IS......

...WORTH SHARING

GOD IS......

... NOT AGEIST

GOD IS....

ALLELUIA!

Amen!

...THE LIFE AND SOUL
OF HIS PEOPLE

GOD IS......

It's no good!—I can't hold it!

... A CONSTANT SUPPORT

GOD IS...

...OFTEN NEGLECTED

GOD IS......

...THE APPLE OF MY EYE

GOD IS...

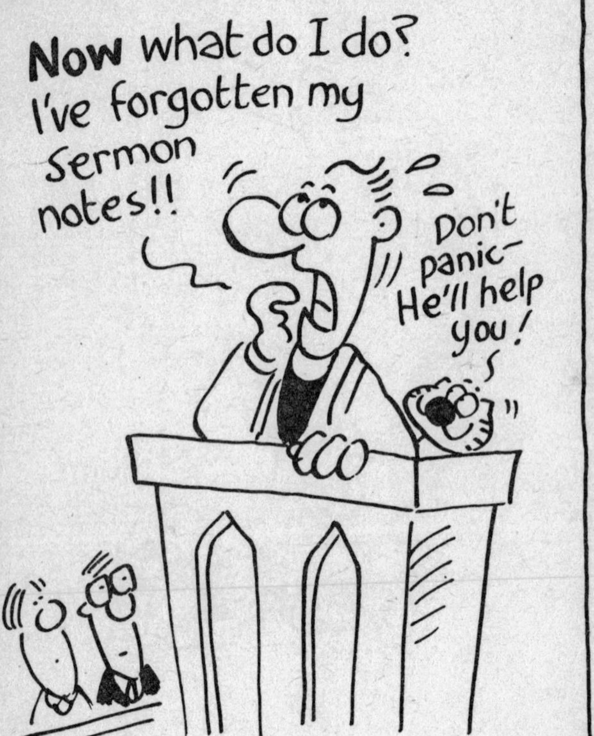

... ABLE TO EQUIP YOU

GOD IS......

... MY SHEPHERD

GOD IS...

...NEVER IN A PANIC

GOD IS....

...THE KEY

GOD IS......

He's around here some- where!

...JUST WHAT YOU'RE LOOKING FOR

GOD IS...

Thank you!! You're wonderful!!!

...WORTHY OF OUR PRAISE

GOD IS....

... STILL LOOKING FOR DISCIPLES

GOD IS........

...TOTALLY SATISFYING

GOD IS....

...NOT JUST FOR SUNDAYS

GOD IS......

... NEVER OUT OF
HIS DEPTH

GOD IS....

... APPROACHABLE

GOD IS......

... SACRIFICIAL

GOD IS...

...THE SOURCE OF JOY

GOD IS......

wow! – this is **amazing!**

...but true!

...TO BE BELIEVED

GOD IS...

... NEVER FORGETFUL

GOD IS.....

...THE $64,000 ANSWER

GOD IS...

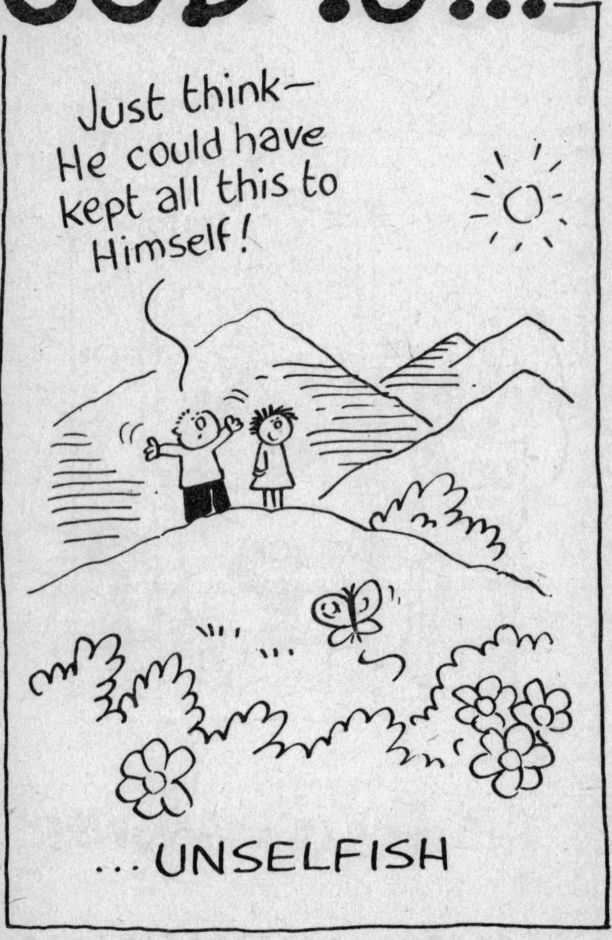

... UNSELFISH

GOD IS......

... BEYOND OUR IMAGINATION

GOD IS...

... FAITHFUL

GOD IS...

... ETERNAL

GOD IS......

nice hat!

... NOT IMPRESSED
BY RANK

GOD IS....

Well.... He's a bit like Dad, but stronger... and He's a bit like Mum, but even gentler... and He's a bit like... er...

... BEYOND COMPARE

GOD IS......

...**REAL** LIFE ASSURANCE

GOD IS....

... THE SUNSHINE OF MY·LIFE

GOD IS...

... BIG-HEARTED

GOD IS...

Give me a break!—
I've only got one
pair of hands!

...and
four
paws!

... **MULTI**-DEXTROUS

GOD IS......

... COMPLETELY
TRUSTWORTHY

GOD IS....

... LIFE TO THE WEARY

GOD IS......

...UNCHANGING

GOD IS.......

...USER-FRIENDLY

GOD IS...

... AN EVER-PRESENT
HELP IN TROUBLE

GOD IS.....

...**NEVER** OUT OF ORDER

GOD IS...

... LOOKING FOR **ACTIVE** SOLDIERS

GOD IS....

... ALWAYS IN TUNE

GOD IS....

... A FRIEND TO THE FRIENDLESS

GOD IS.......

... MORE GENEROUS
WITH US THAN WE
ARE WITH HIM

GOD IS...

... POSSESSIVE

GOD IS...

... ALWAYS WITHIN REACH

GOD IS...

... and you'll never guess what she said then... **well**, she said...

... NOT PLEASED WITH GOSSIP

GOD IS...

... BIGGER THAN WE CAN IMAGINE

GOD IS...

You come on at the end of Act 4, bow, and then get off...

...NOT A BIT PLAYER

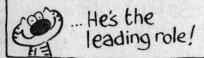

... He's the leading role!

GOD IS...

...THE STRING TO
MY BOW

GOD IS....

...ENVIRONMENTALLY-
FRIENDLY

GOD IS....

... WANTING TO BE **FIRST** IN YOUR LIFE

GOD IS......

...WORTH INVESTIGATING

GOD IS....

... ALWAYS ABLE TO
FIND A WAY OUT

GOD IS.......

...NOT A SOURPUSS!

GOD IS...

I'm **sure** He doesn't mind me fiddling my expenses — I always put 10% of them in the Church collection!

... NOT MOCKED

GOD IS......

... JEALOUS OF
OTHER GODS

GOD IS...

... SOLID AS A ROCK

GOD IS....

... **UN**BREAKABLE

GOD IS......

... ALWAYS UP
BEFORE US

GOD IS....

... ABLE TO DO THE
IMPOSSIBLE

GOD IS......

...PLEASED WHEN WE
ACKNOWLEDGE HIM

GOD IS....

New, **improved** 'WAM' – washes even whiter!!

WAM

but does it remove sin?

...UNIMPROVEABLE

GOD IS...

... NEVER WRONG

GOD IS......

... MYSTERIOUS

GOD IS....

... GOOD NEWS

GOD IS.....

... STRENGTH TO THE WEAK

GOD IS......

... WANTING YOU TO PUT
YOUR LIFE IN HIS HANDS

GOD IS...

Why **should** I loan you my skateboard?— you wouldn't let me use your new bike!

C'mon— forgive and forget!

...NEVER SPITEFUL

GOD IS.......

...ALWAYS UNDERSTANDING

GOD IS....

If you get me a date with that blonde in the typing pool, I'll try to get to church on Sunday...

does she have a cat?

... NOT INTERESTED IN DEALS

GOD IS......

...**IN**DISPENSABLE

GOD IS....

... GOOD

GOD IS......

... SOMETIMES
WANTING US TO CHANGE

GOD IS...
But the forecast was for cold winds and heavy rain!
Who's complaining?
... FULL OF SURPRISES

GOD IS......

... **NEVER** OFF DUTY

GOD IS....

... NEVER STUMPED

GOD IS......

... ABLE TO CLEAN US FROM THE INSIDE

GOD IS......

...ALWAYS IN CONTROL

GOD IS......

...AND YOUR **FUTURE**

GOD IS...

... TRUE TO HIS PROMISES